DANCING ON THE PEDALS

DANCING ON THE PEDALS

The Found Poetry of Phil Liggett, the Voice of Cycling

Edited by Doug Donaldson

BREAKAWAY BOOKS
HALCOTTSVILLE, NEW YORK
2005

Dancing on the Pedals: The Found Poetry of Phil Liggett, the Voice of Cycling

ISBN: 1-891369-55-5
Library of Congress Control Number: 2005920865

Published by Breakaway Books
P.O. Box 24
Halcottsville, NY 12438
(800) 548-4348
www.breakawaybooks.com

FIRST EDITION

NAMESAKE

He's dancing on his pedals

in a most

immodest

way.

Phil's description of Dag Otto Lauritzen climbing
during the 1989 Tour de France

CONTENTS

ACKNOWLEDGMENTS

THANKS . . .
Phil Liggett for his soothing tones,
        deep cycling knowledge, and
        love of the sport.
Bill Strickland for leading me out
        and letting me take the final sprint
        on this book.
Liesa Goins for her sharp editing eyes,
        support, and love.
Keith Gifford for his advice
        and counsel.
Garth Battista and Breakaway for the courage
        to publish such books.
Laura Jorstad for helping each phrase sing with correct
        punctuation and intensely accurate spelling.
World Cycling Productions (www.worldcycling.com)
        for bringing the Tour de France
        and other races to the masses.

And, of course,
Ms. P. C. Franklin for her tireless assistance
        and organizational skills.

A LITTLE PROSE
ABOUT FOUND POETRY

Poetry can be found in all kinds of places—back alley walls, long-forgotten college notebooks, and newspaper headlines. Some have arranged poems from excerpts of technical manuals and quotes from politicians' press conferences. However, the art—the poetry—of Phil is much more than the mere reorganization of words. In the rush of a sprint, the agony of a climb, we become enraptured with the scene, and Phil's words are always part of it all. When we ride, we'll hear Phil's voice encouraging us up a hill or judging just how rubbery our legs have become. When you read his words in the following pages, you might think his free-flowing race descriptions are a little like Jack Kerouac on a mind-altering bike tour. But Phil's words didn't just float out of the thin air of Hautacam; his background and knowledge enable him to not only describe what's happening in front of him, but also tell us where the sport as been and where it'll likely go. His experience, familiarity with the peloton, and love of the sport converge to make each broadcast a verbal work of art. This book attempts to put a pretty frame on those verbal masterpieces. May you have as much joy in Phil's art gallery as I had helping to create it.   —D.D.

PHIL LIGGETT
The Voice of Cycling

Even before Phil Liggett became synonymous with bike racing, he had an impeccable pedigree in the sport. He rode for twelve years as a Category I amateur, raced as a pro in Belgium in 1966, then began writing cycling journalism in 1967. In 1973, he covered his first Tour de France for cycling magazines. He became the youngest commissaire in 1975, judging the world championships in Belgium. The British Broadcasting System hired him to do Tour de France commentary in 1977, and he's been behind the mike ever since. Networks including CBS, ABC, ESPN, and most recently the Outdoor Life Network have also relied on his insider knowledge and smooth delivery to cover the sport. In his home of Britain, he's the president of the seventy-thousand-member CTC cycling club and the technical director of the country's famous Milk Race. Phil is also the author of several books, including *Tour de France*, *The Cycling Year*, *The Complete Book of Performance Cycling*, *The Fastest Man on Two Wheels*, and *Tour de France for Dummies*.

CHAPTER 1

THE GRAND TOUR

History, crowds, and countryside of the world's greatest race

SUMMER ETERNAL

Of course, there's always

a hope

this is the Tour de France

Stage 15, 1998

ON A ROLL

Over the past
few years, especially,
this event
has
delighted,
occasionally
disappointed,
shocked
and
surprised

Stage 1, 2000

ESPRESSO

The riders are now in Bédoin
this is this beautiful town
     with its coffee shops
          where they been sitting
          patiently drinking coffee
          eating their croissants

when we drove through
but not now—that's all left

the Tour de France,
     what they all came to see
          has arrived
               Stage 14, 2002
               Going through Bédoin on the
               way to Mont Ventoux

EIGHT-SECOND WHEELBARROW

Oh dear, Paul,
eight seconds difference
at the halfway mark.

Greg LeMond once won
the Tour de France by eight seconds.
It could be that important.

Prologue, 2004

UNSCRIPTED

The whole Tour
is a surprise
  everything's
gone the way

we would have
  never

     expected

Stage 13, 2003

CALENDAR CHECK

Just a reminder:
Yes, it's supposed to be summer
in France
in the month of July

Stage 7, 1996
On the cold, rainy weather
during the day's stage

YELLOW FIELD

And it wouldn't be a Tour de France,
wouldn't it,
without the sunflowers there

Stage 11, 1999

TASTES LIKE CRÈME BRÛLÉE

The French,
beginning to get the flavor
of their own Tour,
at last

Stage 12, 1994
After three consecutive stage
wins by Frenchmen

DAY, MONTH? JE NE SAIS PAS

The French enjoy the Tour de France.
It gives them a chance
to take a day off.

Stage 10, 1986

RODE HOME

He's thought, well, I'm going to go for it myself
Now he's left it very late
He'll get a lot of cheers here because he's French and he's
such a dapper little man
As he's in his third Tour de France
And his father was a king of the mountains in this race

Stage 15, 2002
About French rider
Miguel Martinez

POOR RICHARD

VUR-Ronk
VEE-Rank
even the French don't know how to say his name

Stage 15, 1997
On French spectators pronouncing
Richard Virenque's name

NO NEUTRALITY

Remember,
we're on the Swiss side now
and they still love the Tour
de France

Stage 16, 1997

STILL LIFE

Many people think:
Why do so many people come to see the Tour de France
when it takes half a minute for the riders to go by on a flat
stage
and about half an hour on a mountain stage?

But, of course, they come because they sample the atmosphere
of this great sporting event
and can follow the rest of it
on television or radio
when it's passed by

Stage 16, 2002

ROAR

They're shouting
because they're saluting
          magnificent athletes
here in the Pyrenees
who have ridden to their maximum
over some of the highest mountains this country has to offer.
One man has proved he is head and shoulders over everyone else,
but they'll continue
to shout everyone home.

> *Stage 13, 2002*
> *On the crowd cheering the riders*
> *following Lance Armstrong*

LE DIFFERENCE

Sometimes the mountains of Italy
are not the same
as the mountains of the Tour de France

> *Stage 14, 2002*
> *On Mont Ventoux*

IN DUTCH

A nasty stinging
in the tail too
for the riders

                              and if you want
                              confirmation
                              we're in Holland,

well, there it is,
even to the flags
on the windmill sails

                              Stage 7, 1992

COALITION OF THE WILLING

It's Spain and America
          as we race across French roads

                         Stage 11, 2002
                         Lance Armstrong, Roberto
                         Heras, and Joseba Beloki on the
                         year's first mountain stage

INDEPENDENCE DAY

Just look at the crowd ahead now as he makes his way up
to the finish
and the cheers
because this is a hometown crowd for the man who just
comes from just the other side.

Those flags, those red flags with the white cross are his
nation's flags
because the Basque people believe they are not Spanish

Stage 14, 2001
On Roberto Laiseka as he
climbs the Luz Ardiden

EASY RIDERS

As the race goes down
far south of the beautiful country,
nobody was in any hurry at all
the peloton dragging
their heels a little bit

Stage 14, 1999

CHAPTER & VERSE

The Tour de France has been written
over these slopes.

Stage 10, 2000

ROLLING THUNDER

This is something special today
the storms that appeared to blow in

blew out

at least as far as the weather is concerned

The storm is all down there
on the highway
today

Stage 14, 2003

PHIL'S DARK HUNGER

Mâcon,

       it's a narrow little village.

In fact, last night, Paul, I was so hungry

       at nearly eleven o'clock

         driving it.

We were hoping we could find a restaurant open.

What a forlorn hope that was.

As we now see it in broad daylight,
it looks like a pleasant place

               Stage 16, 2002
               As the Tour passes through
               Mâcon

LANDSCAPE ASIDE

You see now the area
of deforestation at Mont Ventoux
which was done over four hundred years ago
and it's never recovered and that's another
scarring of our planet by man, but it was done
to build the ships which are made, of course,
of wood those days. Now back to the Tour de France

Stage 14, 2002

STORM FRONT

All of the fears have been realized
 the Col du Galibier is being swept
  by what the French describe as a veritable tempest,
    with winds blowing up to seventy miles
     per hour
      the riders cannot possibly
       cross over the mountain

Stage 9, 1996
On the Tour route being
diverted because of snow.

WEATHER SIGNAL

And, no, we don't need the race conditions, do we?
Just look at them.
Torrential rain and floodwater reported on the roads
as the riders get down to the finish of Aix les Bains
They're all more or less huddled together
and hardly for comfort.
Warnings again of obstacles in the center of the road,
this time the ONCE team sending the signals
a matter of self-survival

> *Stage 6, 1996*
> *About the terrible weather*
> *conditions after Lance*
> *Armstrong abandons*

CLOSE SHAVE

Now, a little bit of a hairy descent here
because there's no fence
there never is in the Alps
as you go downhill

> *Stage 18, 1994*

GRASSY BLUR

Beautiful green countryside
here on the Alps
but the riders don't seem to notice it.
But it really is a lovely area of France

Stage 17, 1994

CAME, SAW, BAKED

They've all come
and they've all died
in the heat today

Stage 9, 1994

MURPHY, THE WEATHERMAN

I shouldn't have mentioned
the weather.

As usual, of course, it does what the commentator says
it won't do.

A bit of a shower
but a heavy storm line
passed.

Stage 3, 2000

WINDOW SHOPPING

What about the man in the overall lead?
He's sat back. He doesn't seem too keen
on trying to stop
　　　these attacks.
Today, as we pass through the usual villages.

Stage 3, 2000

IL PLEUT DANS PHIL'S COEUR

As

we go

off into

the rain again

and slip your

way down

Stage 2, 1992

CHECKPOINT FLAHUTE

It's typically Belgian weather

it's wet and not very nice at all

the border and the police cheering the race

to their side of the country

as you can see no border check here

Stage 6, 1992

NO TIME LIKE THE PRESENT

Whatever did we do without the clocks in the old days?
With the old finger and thumb and stopwatch
       there's no way we can split these riders
       without electronic timing
           these days

Prologue, 2004

BOOM

We can expect
more fireworks
in Paris.

Stage 1, 2000

CHAPTER 2

IN THE PELOTON

Advice, wisdom, and eternal truths about riding the Tour

DAILY DICHOTOMY

Very light winds

                        and very hot indeed

it will be an easy day

                        to destroy yourself

                                Stage 17, 1996

LIBERTY, FRATERNITY & EQUALITY

The Tour de France, you see, is not all flat-out racing.
The riders are as nervous as each other.

                                Stage 11, 1986

THE INNER RACE

No hiding

            now

just flat-out effort

                        and hope

it's good enough

                            Stage 20, 1998
                            Individual time trial

TIMELY REWARDS

You get these chances,
if you take them
when you've lost
time

Stage 15, 2002
On Santiago Botero's breakaway
victory

NEVER TOO LATE

He turned professional at twenty-nine
because he was a truck driver,
  he used to paint them, in fact
And now he's found himself
  as a good bike rider

Stage 11, 1999
On Ludo Dierckxsens during his
solo breakaway

ONE WAY

It is forbidden
to turn around
and go back
to the race.

Stage 12, 2000

SWISS FRANK

Oddly enough,
riders who do ride well in the Tour of Switzerland
very rarely have a great Tour de France

Stage 9, 1996

DOMESTIQUE BLUES

Their job now is very simple:
You race to the limit of your ability.
When you can't do any more,
                you get out
        of the way.

Stage 13, 2002
On the USPS team pulling Arm-
strong to his fourth Tour victory

TRÈS RAPIDEMENT

And this very, very quick Tour
        goes on
                and on
The riders never
seem
to know when
to call
a truce this year.
Under pressure
        all of the time

Stage 13, 1992

BREAKAWAY ETIQUETTE

The important thing
about the Tour de France

to remember
is not to
insist
in a breakaway
like this

if you're not building up
an advantage

on the main field.

Stage 13, 2002

PACE MAKER

If you don't like the day
and you don't like the climbs,
then try and get to the front and ride them at your pace.
And keep everybody
behind
you.

> *Stage 7, 1996*
> *On five-time champion Miguel*
> *Indurain hating the bad weather;*
> *he'll later crack on the stage and*
> *end his string of Tour wins*

POST-APOGEE

This is the one day in a Tour leader's life you hope
        never comes
and you always say it does
        one day

> *Stage 15, 1998*
> *On Jan Ullrich struggling*
> *in bad weather*

ALL THE NEWS FIT TO RIDE

Newspapers up the jersey
keep the wind out
and get ready for the long flight down
no parachutes will be issued

Stage 16, 2002

FALLING WITH STYLE

You can gain
      or lose
   so much time
      going down
        a steep hill.
         It takes a very
           special type of
              man
            with no nerves.

Stage 16, 2000

SOLITUDE

Everyone knows he can climb like an angel.
But to win
the Tour de France
you must be able
to ride well when you're racing
alone
with only yourself
for
company.

Stage 9, 1986
On Robert Millar's individual
time trial

SPRINTER'S RULE

Wiped away now,
the names we talked about
Lance Armstrong, Jan Ullrich
Taking a back seat now
              because this is a matter for the sprinters
You don't get mixed up
now
with the men of steel
      who have no nerves
        who won't win the Tour de France
                    but can win these stages
              Stage 1, 2004
              As Armstrong and Ullrich fade
              back before the bunch sprint

SUNGLASSES AT NIGHT

First attack of the day
Mario Cipollini, who is the Italian playboy,
and although the weather doesn't demand it,
the shades, there, make him look quite a spectacular sight.

He's gained five minutes over a lethargic field.

Stage 7, 1992

DRAFT OR DIE

You can't lead out for the line
and win.

Stage 13, 2002

MOVE DAMMIT!

The riders

                  are supposed to

                              swing off

         when you lead

                    off a man,

not just

        freewheel.

                                Stage 3, 1996

PHOTO FINISH

You have got to be *inch-perfect*

                          to win a sprint

                          Stage 19, 1994

SIMPLE RECIPE

If you can win the time trials
and if you can win the mountains,
there's not much more to win
than the Tour de France.

Stage 9, 1999

ARC DE TRIOMPHE

You're never
      sure of winning
      a Tour de France
      until you get
to Paris.

Stage 15, 1994

CHAPTER 3

ANGRY PEDALS

**Glorious breakaways, searing pain,
and the thrill of competition**

UNITED NATIONS

In that breakaway there's six nations represented
and seven different teams
and with seven teams up there,
it's unlikely that this breakaway will be caught

Stage 12, 1996

BREAK . . .

Look at Tyler Hamilton hanging onto the coattail of
Armstrong
As he continues with his broken collarbone
    if he jumps out of the saddle
    you'll see his face wince with pain
The doctors take him away at night
    they examine him
    and tell him if he's doing any long-term damage
And he comes out of those examinations smiling.

Stage 8, 2003
On Tyler Hamilton riding with
a broken collarbone

. . . AWAY

We thought he'd race for the second
but he's throwing them away
and enjoying the moment

he claps
he believes in himself
he broke his collarbone on Day 2
of the Tour de France
on Stage 16, he's the day's winner

> *Stage 16, 2003*
> *On Tyler Hamilton winning*
> *from a solo breakaway*

CAUSE & EFFECT

A reaction from Ullrich
Now where is Armstrong?
He's got to shut his eyes,

suffer
and grab
that wheel

Stage 13, 2003
Only thirty-seven seconds
separate the two at the time

FASHION DOESN'T KILL

He looks so cool
when he wins.

Stage 4, 1999
On Mario Cipollini, who has
turned in the fastest stage time
to date and will go on to win
four consecutive stages

CADENCE

Up
ahead,
Claveyrolat gains
with every pedal stroke. He's riding
like a man
inspired.

> *Stage 12, 1990*
> *On Thierry Claveyrolat win-*
> *ning the stage on Mont Blanc*

PHAB FIVE

You say it's panic, Paul,
their time is improving since they've lost their men
they've gone through in second place
what they've done now is throw out all their cards
they can't lose anybody else otherwise they've got to stop and
wait

It'll be a big call, but
I think it's just possible, this
as they come up the rise
and make the left turn onto the cobblestones
they could snick it by a couple of seconds

They're going to have to put a bit of a sprint in
but what a turn-up
the problems this team has had on the road
and to produce this ride is absolutely remarkable
and as they come to the line
the clock will give them best time

Stage 4, 2004
On Phonak's team time trial
with just five riders in the last
fifteen kilometers

GAP TO ATTACK

Well, you never know
these boys just will not give up
they've reached the limit of their ability.

They lose contact.

They find the field slows down.
They rejoin
and then they'll say thank heavens I'm back with the leaders.

Then,
     they'll go hit them
               and attack.

Stage 13, 2003

SIX-CYLINDER RESCUE

Armstrong is not the man
of the last four years
               at the moment
and the riders would have searched that out

better than any television commentator

Go Lance, go,
says the clown on the left
He's going well, he's going
                        but not as well
as he normally does

Joseba Beloki is on the attack
and it's up to the others
                        and Armstrong
now, to bring him back

Here comes the cavalry
the U.S. Postal boys are heading the race now
they've got six men down there
and the five men are working for one
They want to launch
Lance Armstrong into the attack

                    Stage 8, 2003
                    On the climb of Alpe d'Huez

PERSEVERE

Here, for me, has been one of the heroes of the day.
If you're ever a cyclist at this level,

> you suffer
>> like Aldag has suffered
>> you are left behind
> you go back to the man
you are left behind again
>> you
>> hang
>> on.

Stage 7, 2003
On Rolf Aldag, struggling
to finish the stage

REIGN FROM SPAIN

This charismatic Basque rider
once had a fan protect him
from the rain with an umbrella
by running alongside him. But
today, Lejarreta needs
no help at all

Stage 14, 1990
About Marino Lejarreta on a
solo break to the stage victory

MORE TIME, PLEASE

Fancy,

  starting with a rider like
    Lance Armstrong
  just two minutes behind

That's a sobering thought

Stage 12, 2003

TIME AND SPACE COLLAPSE

Gaps have gone to question marks
    now,
    on Stuart O'Grady

> *Stage 16, 2002*
> *After slowing during a breakaway*

FACE-OFF

Jean-François Bernard would face
his face
carrying the heaviest load of all
the thirst
of a nation longing for a hero.

> *Stage 10, 1987*
> *On Bernard during the*
> *individual time trial up Mont*
> *Ventoux; he'll finish third in*
> *the Tour*

TANGERINE

Watch out
for the little man in orange

Stage 13, 2002
On David Etxebarria

EAGLE'S REVENGE

Armstrong says you do it to me
            and I'll do it to you
and he's reacted immediately
            and you never ruffle
            the feathers
            of the American

Stage 14, 2002
On Armstrong attacking Joseba
Beloki, who has said he'd attack
the champ

WHERE'S THE KRYPTONITE?

His form is better

than when he won

the Tour de France in 1997

but he's hit a superman

Stage 13, 2001

On Jan Ullrich

SNAPPED ELASTIC

There's Andrea Peron he has been in the break most of the
day
and all of a sudden his legs have gone to rubber
and he slides rather rapidly
out of this group

here

Stage 15, 1999

SUNDAY SPIN

All of the riders are trying
one
on
one
to crack Lance Armstrong
who's sitting there pedaling that low gear
as if he's on a Sunday outing
and he's just watching these riders
destroy themselves right in front of him

Stage 10, 1999
On Alpe d'Huez

SACRIFICIAL LAMB

Now there's a teammate for you,
he's still found the strength
to accelerate

Stage 16, 1998
On Rolf Aldag pulling Jan Ullrich
up the Col de la Madeleine

COPPI ASIDE

They used to laugh at Claudio Chiappucci
and they don't laugh at him any more
if we had ten Claudio Chiappuccis in the Tour de France,
I don't think there would be more than ten finishers
this rider never knows when to stop racing.

And don't forget the magnet of his home country
now he's being drawn toward Sestriere
> 1952 the Tour de France ended in Sestriere with a stage
> and the winner then none less than Fausto Coppi,
> in many people's eyes the greatest cyclist who ever lived
and Coppi would be delighted at the way this young man is
> taking riders
on the Tour de France today.

Stage 13, 1992
Chiappucci will go on to win
king of the mountains and second
in the general classification

IN THE PIRATE'S WAKE

It appeared initially he was coming back
but looks to me as though he's not
    just cracked physically,
    he's cracked mentally here
and the way he's dropped
back
he's a very lonely rider, indeed
nobody around to help him
and his Tour de France is running away from him
and I didn't think we'd be saying that this year

Stage 15, 1998
As Marco Pantani rides away
from Jan Ullrich

POLKA-DOT NOD

Ullrich has played
the honest soldier
there
and allowed Virenque
his win in the Alps

Stage 14, 1997

AFTER THE DAM BREAKS

He still has a fine turn
of speed
in those legs

But not

to hold off the whole
of the Tour de France
today
As the riders
come together

Stage 5, 1996
On Viatcheslav Ekimov taking
a flier in the last few kilometers

GET THE POINT

Virenque, here,
>   fighting for third
Indurain chasing
>   he won't give him an inch, either
>   for Richard Virenque going for the points.
And can you believe that?
Indurain takes the points off him
>   and stares him straight in the face.
Well, that was a little slap over the wrist, I think,
>   for Richard Virenque
>   because Indurain didn't have a real interest in the
king of the mountains

> *Stage 17, 1994*
> *On Indurain robbing Virenque*
> *of king of the mountains points*

BIG LUMPS

One hundred twenty-eight riders left.
They're falling out
     in big lumps
     every day

Stage 17, 1994

THE EDGE

They know exactly
what they have to do.
They are the sharp end of the race.

Stage 12, 2000

MARQUEE FATIGUE

I've never seen so many tired
BIG NAMES
in the Tour de France for years.
These fellas have all tried and been destroyed.

Stage 10, 2000

AS SWEET AS A PATISSERIE

His legs are not strong enough
> to pedal the highest gear on that bike
> although the road is flat.

They are so tired after sixty miles in the lead today.

But Jalabert is getting ready for the two-arm victory salute
> and this will be sweet.

Bastille Day in France and a Frenchman comes home.

There aren't many who can claim that
> and this man will have done it twice.

Stage 7, 2001
On Laurent Jalabert's stage win

PACK ZEN

The field
is coming
> so
> so
> fast.

Stage 9, 2000

SHARP EFFICIENCY

Delgado's disc wheels
slice through the still air.
He puts every ounce of strength
into going quickly.

Stage 5, 1989
On Pedro Delgado's individual
time trial; he will finish third
in the Tour

ANTICIPATION

Is he going to build on that?
Or is he going to slow down?
Is he?
And he isn't.

Stage 1, 2000
On Jan Ullrich dropping
behind the individual time trial
stage winner David Millar's
time

PACK IT IN

There's
going
to be
nobody
left on
this climb
very shortly.
There's so many riders
getting dropped they're
going to reform in a big bunch.

Stage 13, 2002

NIGHTMARE

He goes to bed tonight dreaming of what might have been.
He's gone a little too soon.

Stage 13, 2000
On Didier Rous attacking too
soon to try to win the stage on
Bastille Day

3X

That is a triple Dekker.
This is how
he's done it—with his mouth wide open.

Stage 17, 2000
On Erik Dekker's stage win

GONE

As he kicks
NOW
All
or
nothing.

Stage 18, 2000
On stage winner Salvatore
Commesso's counterattack in a
breakaway forty-two kilometers
before the line

GREAT ESCAPE

Oh dear me,
look at the face now of Claudio Chiappucci
because he's on the last climb,
this is the climb up to Sestriere itself.
Surely, he's not going to crack now
this has been an escape of magnitude.
Some 190 kilometers in the lead so far
for Claudio Chiappucci
      and this will go in the history books
      as one of the great escapes of the Tour de France of
modern times

And Indurain knows it, too.

Stage 12, 1992

BOTTOM LINE

The race is
no respecter
of reputation.
You're only
as good as
now.

Stage 15, 1988
On Charly Mottet abandoning

WORLD OF HURT

LeMond in desperate trouble again
just as he was in the Pyrenees one year ago
LeMond is going backwards today
      and backwards very, very quickly indeed
and that is a sad sight
I think Greg, secretly you know, has been worried
about these mountains coming

Each day, he's tried throughout this Tour de France to gain time
        on the flatter stages to gain time
to get himself a better springboard into the Alps
        and it hasn't come

And this is the rider who is destroying Greg LeMond today
        Claudio Chiappucci,
        second in the Tour de France last year,
        second in the last two years in the Tour of Italy
he's attacked virtually at the drop of the flag today
and now he's
        tapping out
        the rhythm
        all
        by himself

                    Stage 13, 1992
                    Eighteen riders will abandon
                    during the stage

SHADES OF AGONY

Now the face of Miguel Indurain
wearing glasses today
so you can't see
what his eyes are obviously feeling
because there's pain
in those eyes today.

Stage 16, 1993

CRITICAL CHARGE

Delgado is in the lead. He's annoyed
at an overly enthusiastic fan,
and angrily accelerates. Delgado charges
toward what he thinks will be a magnificent victory.
A reply to all this critics. But
Millar inches his way back to Delgado. Now
you see why Millar is known
as the Man of the Pyrenees.

Stage 10, 1989
On the Pedro Delgado and
Robert Millar duel

THREE-ACT PLAY ON ALPE D'HUEZ

I.

Well, I don't think Ullrich believes it either
Armstrong has given everybody,
and maybe that was the plan to give everybody,
the impression that he was in trouble

II.

Look at the face of Ullrich
as Armstrong has found his wheel
A good reply by Ullrich
and this is going to be a mano a mano now
and this has really happened before
the climb has started

III.

A big move by Lance,
This
and there's no reply coming at all from Jan Ullrich
Ullrich has got no answer
to this acceleration by Lance Armstrong

He took a look straight into the eyes there of Jan Ullrich
        and said:
        Well here I go, are you coming or not?

        And the answer is
        NOT.

Today, Armstrong gave them a big start
        and ripped them apart

                                Stage 10, 2001
                                On the Alpe d'Huez climb

CHAPTER 4

INTO THE BARRIERS

Spectacular crashes, devastating falls, and near-misses

PAST

Riders fall and need
wheels replaced
by helpers from their team cars.
Dust gets into the riders'
lungs as much.
But still,
the speed of the race
is relentless.

Stage 4, 1989

SLIDING LEAD

He was in the lead
      by about six seconds
when he fell

We can look at this now:
This is the grease on the roundabout
      and they saw the sparks flying

Stage 19, 2003
On Jan Ullrich falling during
the individual time trial

HEADSTONE

Sadness of the days gone by
In northern France
with the gravestones of all of the cemeteries
that abound in this area.

The touch of wheels, there, and that was Alonso who went down
and I think you know he clipped his head on the roadside there
well, as you may know
crash helmets are not compulsory
in professional cycling in Europe
it's a matter of personal choice

and Alonso here might have required one
because he has hurt his head

Stage 5, 1992
On Marino Alonso's crash

FROM THE ASHES

Oh, there's been a crash!
A major pileup, there, as the riders go through!

But keep your eyes on the front
because Robbie McEwen is taking it
McEwen always comes out best
when the going gets rough
Hushovd is the new Maillot Jaune
                    of the Tour de France
                              McEwen gets
                    the result
and he leaves
          behind
      the debris
                    Stage 2, 2004

HOOKED

Ohhhhhhhh!
What has happened there?
It seemed quite a normal corner.
He must have hit somebody in the audience.

Mayo has gone.

Stage 15, 2003
On Armstrong falling on the
Luz Ardiden climb

DELICATESSEN

There's a big sandwich out there
and a very nasty fall.

Stage 3, 2003

HAYRIDE

It's a left hand corner
completely out of control.
                There's no way
he was going anywhere.

He locks up
his back wheel,

Well, thank heavens there was a straw bale there
That's called a headstand
        in front
        of the
        public

Stage 7, 1999
On Abraham Olano during the
individual time trial

COUNT YOUR BLESSINGS, JENS

This was Jens Voigt
And this is the way to lose
      your king of the mountains jersey
He was lucky that's all he's lost

Stage 10, 1998

BIKE TOSS

Well this is unbelievable.
This has not been Riis's day
and there's about $7,000 worth of machine
      that has been hailed across the road there.

Bjarne Riis actually fell off when he came to sign up
for the start
and then reported and got a twenty-second-late departure.
Now, he's had a flat out on the course.

Stage 20, 1997

CONSTRICTION

And there's a crash down there
and look at the way the peloton
is spread round in a big circle
> crossing
> a narrow
> bridge
and this is another bit of confusion
riders falling as they have been daily in this race
taking out one or two of the stars as well

Stage 5, 1996

ORANGE MONSTER

Thank heavens for the barriers
which is more than you can say for Abdoujaparov
a few years ago
when he hit them at the finish of a stage in Paris

Stage 4, 1996

BEND, NOT BREAK

The back wheel of Indurain
he lost it there
Indurain is going around this corner
                              out of control
And he's just locked up the back wheel
to get around
it's a nasty squeeze.

Well, that's the closest Indurain must have come
to falling off.

Stage 15, 1994

FAIR WARNING

Oh! Look at this!
Oh! My goodness me!
That was the roundabout
we were warned about.
And they've gone straight on into the barriers.

Stage 4, 1995

ARMOIRE SALE

Two tricky little bends: That's traffic furniture
on French streets.

Stage 3, 2000

PINBALL

A ricochet crash
a touch of wheels in the middle.

Stage 3, 2000

REBOUND

Great courage
      and sense
to get back on
the bike
and save
      the day.

Stage 3, 2000
On David Millar's crash

BROKEN WING

He's come in
all the way
to the finish
with his arm draped
over the bar
unable
to steer.

Stage 6, 2000
On Stuart O'Grady finishing
the stage with an injured arm

HAIRPINNED

Watch
as he goes
around this corner—
one of the steepest corners.
Ouch.

Stage 12, 2000

DNF REDEUX

The crashes are continuing
and this looks like it's Fabio Parra on the ground
this is absolutely amazing
history repeating itself here
because Parra crashed out last year—
a bridge in the north of France
and it was a bridge that caused the crash again
and right on the side of the road too

I'm afraid the way Parra is nursing himself
he's broken his ribs here

And that is very, very sad indeed
the Colombian is out of the Tour de France
and very likely his final Tour de France

Stage 8, 1992

ICED VEINS

A glacial descent
And this is Massimiliano Lelli
just about staying on the road there

                        and only just
                        Stage 1, 1992

RERUN

Oh, my goodness me!
They've hit the policeman!
They've all come down!
That is a terrible crash!

That is an amazing pile.

Watch this again.

                        Stage 1, 1994

CHAPTER 5

UP TO HEAVEN

Legendary climbs, mountaintop finishes, and the polka-dot jersey

INQUISITION

It's only a mountain,
one of many you can see
on this French country morning
but for one hundred seventy-one young men
it would be a place
where they would dare
to ask themselves
the questions
of greatness

Stage 10, 1987
On an Individual time trial up
Mont Ventoux, one of the most
grueling stages in Tour history

ASK & RECEIVE

Well, the riders (at least some of them)
said they wanted more mountains
well, they've got the more mountains
this year. Two very tough days here.

Stage 10, 1993

WEEP

Now Virenque,
I'm not sure whether he's crying here through joy
or through pain
but either way, I'm sure it'll be joy in a few minutes' time
he's just got the last few corners to go
and he's really into the heart of crowd now
the heart and soul of Luz Ardiden

Stage 12, 1994
On Richard Virenque's stage
win at Luz Ardiden

SLOW FALL

There's no reason to hurry
on this climb as long
as you keep the tempo
at the right speed
the riders will fall back.

Stage 11, 1993

VERACITY DISTILLED

The mountains again
have produced the truth,
and produced two
great men

Stage 18, 1986
On Greg LeMond and Bernard
Hinault's battle on Alpe d'Huez

DEMYSTIFIED

All of the great winners
of the Tour de France
win at Alpe d'Huez.
It is the shrine, the mecca of the race,
of the world of cycling indeed.
It used to be the domain of the Dutch
but now, just about everyone
        with a fine pair of racing legs
        is getting in on the action.

Stage 10, 2001

HABERDASHERY

It's a strange climb,
the Col de la Bonette
It really is like the shape of a hat,
because the riders climb to the top
and they go round the side of the bonnet
and then they descend away down to the left of our
        picture
back down the bottom
and the finish before they have to climb, of course,
to Isola 2000
that's a climb the Tour de France has never before gone up
and it's very, very steep

Stage 11, 1993

PINCH NEZ

No one will
do anything
in the valley
because of the long climb
on their noses.

Stage 13, 2000
On the Côte de Cadarache

FLIGHT CONTROL

The old legs
have gone now,
they're on automatic pilot
now

Stage 14, 2002
On Richard Virenque climbing
Mont Ventoux

GUTS

And so the Tour de France is in the mountains
for the first time and, my goodness me,
what a day already it has been. This Tour de France,
about to be turned inside
out.

Stage 12, 1986

GRIT

Nobody anxious now
to the first rendezvous with the big climb in the Pyrenees,
the Col de la Marie Blanc

Stage 2, 1992

GRIM

It's the only day
the riders are in the Pyrenees,
and they are
far from happy.

Stage 10, 2000

GRIN

All the riders smiling

now

as they leave the Pyrenees behind.

Stage 16, 1999

SHUTTLE SERVICE

Isn't that beautiful.

That's the road.

They're coursing along around the edge of the mountain now.

This man is off that road and into *the* mountain today.

There's only one way out of this tour now

      that's back down the road he's climbing up

but

      he'll be doing that by car later.

Stage 16, 2002
On Michael Boogerd's breakaway

TOUGH CROWD

The crowd is getting extremely twitchy at the finishing line.

I've never seen a crowd like this on the climb of Mont
Ventoux

    as Richard Virenque races to the top now as if drawn
like a magnet to the pole.

He is going up toward the summit, a fully deserving stage
winner today.

He's done it the hard way.

He must earn the applause of everyone.

Stage 14, 2002

SPANKING

The big daddy,

    the Col de la Madeleine

        at the end

        of the stage

Stage 16, 1998

WATCH FOR FALLING ROCKS

He descends like a stone
he'll get back to those three
if he doesn't overdo it
and let's hope he doesn't do that
come on Walter, you can see the summit
now one big effort and you're over the top and you're less
than a minute behind
and you descend better than those three men in front of you
if he won, that would be unbelievable

Stage 14, 2003
On Walter Bénéteau, who will
finish fifth on the day

PRAYER

This man is head-bowed.
He can't believe
　　　　it goes
　　　　on
　　　　and on
　　　　and on.

Stage 16, 2002
On Michael Boogerd winning
the stage to La Plagne

PARADISO

This is the wonderful moment
when you come alone to the summit of Alpe d'Huez.
Time, at this minute, is not important
when you're winning the stage at Alpe d'Huez,
it's all about success.

Stage 8, 2003
On Iban Mayo's stage win

PURGATORIO

And then,
they'll be in the shadow
of the Pyrenees.

Stage 9, 2000

INFERNO

There's our friend
the devil
who's joined us
the past few days.

Stage 11, 1994
On the climb up Hautacam

PAIN BY ANY OTHER NAME

In a few minutes time, we'll see the first numbered bend
which should be No. 18

as we start the climb up this mountain
and each one has a name.
And it 'tis a rather cruel thing

I don't know whether they've taken the idea from
Alpe d'Huez, which has always had numbered hairpin bends,
but here they've named every one as well.
It just tells you how far you've got to climb.

If you're suffering,
I would think you wouldn't want
to see that.

Stage 16, 2002
On the climb up La Plagne

BLAME THE MECHANIC

I don't think he had a mechanical problem
I think he just got the steeper parts of Ventoux
and felt the pace
too much

Stage 14, 2002
On Francisco Mancebo's ascent

OUTER SPACE

Then the last couple kilometers
they break out
on the moon

Stage 14, 2002
On Mont Ventoux

REARVIEW MIRROR

As he goes 'round the corner looks
down
the valley
to see where they are now
he knows they are coming,
         he knows they are coming
Quickly he can pedal.

And my goodness me, when you break away after
         twenty-seven kilometers
and you're still leading with just six kilometers to go
his legs must be terribly, terribly tired.

But he is the new king of the mountains
and what a king he is!

Stage 13, 2001
On Laurent Jalabert

TEETH MARKS

I.

Ullrich is being dragged
very quickly
by the scruff of the neck
back into this pack
because the climb is already
starting to bite.

Stage 11, 1998

II.

Now
is where Mont Ventoux
starts to bite.

Stage 12, 2000

GAMBIT ACCEPTED

Hardly looking across at the Pirate
but he's trying to visually lift his pace
      he knows the acceleration is coming

Here it comes now from Pantani
Such a typical attitude of a climber,
      lift the tempo
           one more notch

And simply break
your rival

Stage 11, 1998
On the Plateau de Beille

HIGH KU

Last day in the Alps
and it's been a real sort-out—
the men from the rest

Stage 11, 1993

SAILS UNFURLED

Look at that
for a gap

Pantani has opened it up

But this plucky little rider Richard Virenque
        is afraid of no one this year
        he's come again
        he's really proud to wear the polka-dot jersey
                as king of the mountains
        and he's going to come after Pantani

But whether he's got the legs,
I don't know

Stage 16, 1994
On the Alpe d'Huez

SPIN CYCLE

The riders have to stand
on the pedals
as the grade gets steeper and steeper.
In the early part of this century
when these mountains' roads were unpaved,
riders were forced to walk over summits. Endurance
and stamina were the keys to success in those days.
Speed
and aerobic fitness
are now more important.

Stage 10, 1989

YES, BOSS

Great climbers,
men who can so easily win races
in their own right, they have to succumb
to the domesticity
of helping their team
leaders.

Stage 11, 1993
On Isola 2000 and Col de la Bonette

HAPPY ENDING

A poor start to the Alps
        might be a great finish
for Claudio Chiappucci

Stage 11, 1993

CHOO-CHOO

See!
And the train is leaving the station
and the man who's going to miss it
is Andy Hampsten

Stage 11, 1993

PITCHFORK & ALL

They've tamed the devil
and he's riding no-handed
in third place

Stage 11, 1993
On Jenon Jaskula riding
behind Indurain

ONE SHOT

With three miles of the Tourmalet remaining,
the Swiss champion is dropped.
There are no second chances
on such a long,
difficult climb.

Stage 10, 1989
On Pascal Richard dropping
from the break

BEAST

Vicious
is the word.
Savage
is the climb.

Stage 12, 2000
On Mont Ventoux

TASTE OF VICTORY

Just what is Indurain thinking now.
He's got one rider ahead of him
Marco Pantani

And Indurain with all the time in hand he requires
is now trying to go for gold, I think
here on the first day in the Pyrenees.

This will have a nice taste about it
in the mountains.

Stage 11, 1994
On the duel up Hautacam

RAREFIED

The man of the day
there's no doubt who that is
Andy Hampsten
has pulled off the ride of his life there
and thank heaven the organization has held the crowd back
because you need all the air you can get
when you climb to the top of Alpe d'Huez

Stage 14, 1992

HAZING

These slopes aren't
steep
enough. It gets worse.

Stage 12, 2000

WHAT'S UP DOC?

That is probably why Richard Virenque has been told
to go out early on the attack.
Well, he's the carrot for the rest to follow.
We climb up again toward the skyline here
and Virenque is stepping out
the message.

Stage 15, 1993

ADIEU

It is a long, long difficult climb
This is a hard way to say good-bye to the Alps

Stage 16, 1997

CHAPTER 6

PULLING ON THE MAILLOT JAUNE

Legend, lore, and the pursuit of the Yellow Jersey

COVET

The Maillot Jaune
everybody wants it,
and when you've got it, everybody can't keep it.

Stage 9, 1996

TURNING ON THE TAP

The arrival of the Yellow Jersey is imminent
There's anger in that face and concentration
He's reliving his training days from a couple months ago
         He knows every hole in this road

Stage 16, 2002
On Lance Armstrong on the
La Plagne climb after
breaking away

COME TO PARIS

The

Eiffel

Tower

didn't throw

a shadow

over this   race for

the man   in Yellow

Stage 23, 1986

WHEN A BADGER ISN'T A BADGER

I've seen fourteen Tours de France and
I can honestly say I've never seen
riders attack the Yellow Jersey like this.
Which means: They all believe
that Bernard Hinault
is not the man he led
us to believe,
today.

Stage 13, 1986

PREDESTINATION

He had no choice.
He had to win.

> *Stage 15, 2004*
> *On Armstrong winning on the*
> *line, taking Yellow for first time*
> *this year*

BORN AGAIN

This man lives to fight again.
The Tour de France hero in the first days,
      he's going to keep his Yellow.
You won't believe the crowd here.
They're cheering him like a winner of the Tour de France.
He's riding up now for a Maillot Jaune.
After two vicious days in the Pyrenees.
We thought three hours ago it was all over
for Thomas Voeckler.
Now in the next minute, he'll still be in the Yellow Jersey.
He's going to watch,
      he's going to get there.

> *Stage 13, 2004*
> *On the Plateau de Beille*

BRINGING IT HOME

I.

The crowd are cheering along the barriers all the way.
The moment every Frenchman dreams of very few have it.
He'll be only the eighty-second Frenchman ever to pull on
     the Maillot Jaune
as he races up toward the line, now, he looks at the crowd
he gives them a smile,
he gives them a grit of his teeth
he's still looking for that banner.
When is it going to come?
This is a rather nasty little hill up to the line,
     the way they come up these days
This wasn't the way he came up in the year 2000.
Almost exactly the same salute when he arrived here in 2000
     Richard Virenque takes Stage 7 of the Tour de France
     the clock starts now and he is looking for Yellow.

Stage 7, 2003

II.

But the man signaling at the back is Richard Virenque.
He knows now he is the new leader of the Tour de France
and *that* is important
especially when you're a Frenchman
bringing the race into Pau into France for the first time.
And look at this.
This is Richard Virenque
and the tears say it all,
the proudest moment of his young life.
He says I've got the Maillot Jaune,
        the Yellow Jersey
and there's proof of that.

Stage 2, 1992

GONE, BABY, GONE

Seven days in Yellow.
It's all but a dream now.

Stage 11, 2002
On Igor Gonzalez de Galdeano
after losing the Maillot Jaune

MOTIVATION

This has been the finest team trial ever by Crédit Agricole.
They have been inspired by the Golden Fleece.
They will keep the race lead and with the best time of the day.

Stage 5, 2001
On Crédit Agricole beating
U.S. Postal in the team time
trial

TONGUE TWIST

Elli in Yellow.
Be careful
how you say that.

Stage 7, 2000
On Alberto Elli

GREEN, NO YELLOW

This is come
to a sprint
to the line
here
to win
and take
the leader's
Yellow.
It's all on.

Stage 1, 2000

ROOM SERVICE

The Yellow Jersey will go to his hotel,
tonight,
his room.

Stage 10, 2000

DEUX HOMMES

Once
you pull on
that Golden Fleece
you become
two men.

Stage 17, 1996
On Bjarne Riis attacking
in Yellow

ONE OF THOSE DAYS

What a day
this has turned out to be
the king of the mountains
                    has been dropped
we have seen the Yellow Jersey
                    abandoned
we know of one

            bad crash

Stage 7, 1996
On Abraham Olano during
the individual time trial

YOUNG PROFESSIONAL

Immediately,
this is an attack by Richard Virenque
nnother rider in his first Tour de France,
>   second year professional,
>   well, third season actually now
and he's actually now trying to break clear of the field
and he's starting to build up quite a lead here
the object is the Yellow Jersey
he's riding very, very well on the hills
>   and he's challenging for the lead too of king
>   of the mountains

Stage 2, 1992

CHAPTER 7

HALL OF CHAMPIONS

**Triumph, defeat, and a salute
to the winners of the Tour**

BIG RING

There goes Bernard Hinault
in a gear
most men use
only
on the
downhills

> *Stage 10, 1985*
> *On the brutal attack Hinault launches*
> *to stake his claim on his fifth Tour*
> *victory*

VICIOUS TEETH

And so the Badger has come out
of its corner
once again
to take on
all the riders at the Tour de France

> *Stage 12, 1986*
> *On Hinault attacking to put himself in*
> *Yellow by the end of the stage, but he*
> *will lose this Tour to Greg LeMond*

SPECTACLE

Fignon detests the rain
as it fogs up
his glasses. Yet
he still rides
with power.

Stage 5, 1989
On Laurent Fignon's trademark
wire-rimmed glasses during the
individual time trial

OVER LE HUMP

Look at the rhythm being taped out
       on the slopes here of the Grand Ballon
and that's why Fignon has gone

clear

Fignon now is free as a bird on the climb Grand Ballon
well there's still some fifty kilometers to go once he's over
and that banner is inspiration
to the Frenchman

           Stage 11, 1992
           On Fignon's stage win

GREG LEMOND

RED, WHITE, BLUE & YELLOW

America was watching
and the young American
was home on the cobblestones
of the Champs-Elysées.

Stage 23, 1986
On LeMond's first Tour victory

WHAT'S FOR DINNER?

Back in the field, there,
nobody one seems concerned about the crashes.
Greg LeMond seems more concerned
about what he ate last night.
Greg LeMond talking about
one of his favorite foods,
Chinese and Mexican

Stage 8, 1992

PAPARAZZI

Greg LeMond, well, as ever
climbing up to fifth overall now
and the press is annoying him at the finish.
Greg LeMond as always the hottest property
in world cycling,
even if he didn't win the Tour de France
and the only way of escape—
over the barriers and into the safety
of underneath this truck.
He's asking a little bit of time
to get changed.

Stage 6, 1992

BOTTOM TO TOP

For Stephen Roche
the cheers of the crowd would echo
his response to the mountain.
As a seven-year-old
he earned the money for his first bicycle
by sweeping Dublin
floors.

Stage 10, 1987
On the individual time trial up
Mont Ventoux

ON TIME

A year ago,
Stephen Roche had been disqualified

for missing

the start of the team time trial.
What a difference a year makes.

Stage 4, 1992

IN MEMORIAM

Roche has no answer
to a man driven
by such emotion.

Stage 19, 1987
On Pedro Delgado's stage victory
on the anniversary of his
mother's death

WAKE-UP CALL

Start time arrives
for Delgado, the defending
champion.
But where is he?
He's throwing away time.

Prologue, 1989
On Delgado being 2:44 late
for the start

SPANISH FLIER

That is amazing
now he hits the cobble hill
and dances
is dancing away too
to big gains
in the Tour de France today

Stage 9, 1992
On Indurain's individual
time trial

SMOOTH CATCH

And indeed,
Indurain has just gone
straight up to him
with all the ease of a champion.
And that's all
he wanted to do
as well.   *Stage 11, 1993*

SOUND SCALE

Look at the cheers
now
for Indurain, the faces
these people.
They've waited
for days to see Indurain
climb this mountain.
Now
they're cheering him up
through a corridor
of noise.

Stage 11, 1994
On Indurain's climb up
Alpe d'Huez

PEARLY WHITES

This is going to be a big emotional moment
for a big man
And he can afford to smile

Stage 15, 1994

THE SLIP

Indurain has been dropped here
This is not
the going-forward part of the group,
this is the going-backward part of the group

Stage 7, 1996
On his thirty-second birthday

LEADER ON THE ROAD

To win a stage like this when you wear the Maillot Jaune
To look at the riders and blow them off
one by one
off your wheel
you know you are the very best.

Stage 16, 1996
On Riis's stage win

JAN ULLRICH

AS SEEN ON TV
This rider has never
seen the Tour de France
           only on television
and look at him now

Stage 9, 1996

PREVIEW
Another fine ride
by this youngster,
           the 1993 amateur champion
           a great sprinter,
           a great time trialist
           and a great climber
All the qualities you need to one day
win the Tour de France

Stage 16, 1996

FORESHADOW

I.

He looks back
to see
who's chasing. The answer
is no one.

Stage 10, 1997
On Ullrich's solo breakaway

II.

And Ullrich looks
behind him, goodness
knows why, because the whole
of the Tour de France is in
front of him

Stage 12, 1997
On Ullrich's individual
time trial

TIE A PORK CHOP AROUND HIS NECK

Once again
Jan Ullrich is finding out
that the Tour de France is
not his friend.

Stage 15, 1998

LICKED

The face of Jan,
licking lips, the climb ahead.

Stage 13, 2000

WORD UP

This man doesn't know the word
"I'm giving up"

Stage 14, 2001

SELF-FULFILLING SISYPHUS

He is the classiest bike rider in the world,
but there are times he lets himself down.
If he's come back, well,
hats off to him.

Prologue, 2003

VIVA MARCO

I think I can just see
the white jersey
of Pantani
through the mist.

Stage 11, 1994

AGITATOR

He annoys everybody
  with the way he attacks
    and his accelerations are fabulous
        Pantani going
           clear
              now

Stage 17, 1994

SHORN CAESAR

Now they welcome
again
an Italian conqueror
of the Alps

Stage 15, 1997
On Pantani's stage win

PLUNDER

I.

Conditions here on the Galibier are quite atrocious now
we're going up to the highest point
of this year's Tour de France
and Pantani isn't going to wait
we're a long way from the top
and a long way from the finish here
and nobody is reacting

II.
The little man
        has danced
once again
        to the summit

Stage 15, 1998
On Pantani finishing nine
minutes in front of the leader
after the Col du Galibier

CONTENDER

He is settling in.
He is recovering.
And he will kick in.

Stage 14, 2000

LANCE ARMSTRONG

ONCE UPON A TIME

Armstrong has been washed away a little bit.

But Armstrong is coming back.
This could be a fairy-tale
entry into his first Tour de France.
Armstrong is through
and the young American, the youngest man in the race,
in fact Lance Armstrong has won
his stage
in the Tour de France at Verdun.
And look how easily he did it

Stage 8, 1993

PAST PRESENT

He is riding like
the halcyon days
of Eddy Merckx.

Stage 18, 1995
On Armstrong's solo break the
day after teammate Fabio
Casartelli's death

ANY MORE QUESTIONS?

After his time trials everyone said,
        "Oh yes, but how about the mountains?"
Well, here's the answer now
because Armstrong has ridden the mountains
better than anyone else.

Stage 9, 1999

FIGHTING WORDS

Armstrong didn't start
it.
But he's going to
finish it.

Stage 10, 2000

NO HYPE

Superlatives
simply
don't describe
just how
he rides a bike

Stage 13, 2002

BLUE CRUSH

I.

This is another attack
and we've seen this on the mountains
around France the past few weeks
and now he's gone again
and when he goes, Paul, we wonder
because this man just opens the gap
and makes Ullrich look like a club cyclist

II.

Lance Armstrong has flown

away

from the Tour de France

III.

Dancing away to this third stage victory
of this year's Tour de France is Lance Armstrong.
Free as a bird to fly now.

He's crossed all of the cols.

He's been attacked and counter-attacked.

He's had to come back.

He's even waited for Jan Ullrich when he fell off

And now mano a mano he just flies away.

Stage 13, 2001

THE LAST CHASE

Lance, now,

has no rivals

except

the race itself

Stage 16, 2004
On the climb up Alpe d'Huez

CHAPTER 8

THE FINISHING LINE

**Long leadouts, slim margins,
and the rush to the end**

CAUGHT IN 1K

How cruel
>
>   is life
>
>   as a pro bike rider?

As the sprinters now look to reassess up here

Stage 4, 2003

CHOPSTOCKS

They cannot afford to mess around.

It's a slightly uphill finish.

If you wait you're dead,

>   because the peloton are on your tail
>
>   and it's a big leadout now.

Stage 9, 2004
On the Iñigo Landaluze and
Filippo Simeoni breakaway that
will be caught just meters
before the line

ON TRACK

He's got the biggest man to hide behind.
This could be a perfect finish.
Stuart O'Grady is a pure man.
It's a track finish, this.
He's the ace rider on the track.
He's won medals there
      at every color
      commonwealth and world championship.
Now goes Sandy Casar, is he going to upset it?
Now comes O'Grady on the inside.
O'Grady takes his teeth and takes on Casar.
Nobody will beat O'Grady in a finish like this
The Australian remembers 1998,
      takes it on the line.

Stage 5, 2004
As O'Grady wins the sprint,
barely beating Sandy Casar
and Jakob Piil

EMERGENCY CALL

They're all together again in the breakaway
Telekom are looking for more help from other riders.
They seem to have given their all and they haven't got a lot left.
This is going to be a desperate
      finish here now.

Stage 20, 1993

THE LONGEST KILOMETER

When is a thousand meters longer than a thousand meters?
When you're riding the Tour de France and winning on your
    own
      but the peloton is chasing you down—
      a bunch of riders in this case.
And he's checking, checking, checking...
Because he's got no more speed left in those legs and will that
banner ever come toward him here?
He wants a long time to enjoy himself.

Stage 11, 2003
On Juan Antonio Flecha's solo win

THE GREEN MACHINE

Erik Zabel

looks over

his shoulder

as he has done

the past three days

Stage 20, 2001
On Zabel winning his sixth
Green Jersey

DUEL DÉNOUEMENT

He's got to go sooner or later.

And it's just like you're in a velodrome here

high on the banking

because the rider on the front is just turning his neck to wait

for the move

and hopes he can beat him by a fraction of a second.

But here it comes and I don't think he's got a chance.

He's gambling on a quick release

as he comes up to his back wheel a quick deep breath

and then can he take him
and Fabio Sacchi is racing to what would certainly be the
biggest result of his life
and watch out Jakob Piil is finding the legs to the line
and that is a tremendous result for Jakob Piil
He did turn on the style.
He led to the line he forced Sacchi to make the move.

Stage 10, 2003
As Jakob Piil takes Fabio Sacchi
on the line after the two were
away with fifteen kilometers to go

INSIDE OUT DOWN UNDER

Robbie McEwen has taken
the Green Jersey
in the finest
possible
manner.
And I think he's crying.

Stage 20, 2002

THE LION RETURNS

Cipollini
is towing
the best sprinters
to the line but they'll never
get by this man
when he has
such a clear shot
at the finish line.
He's being challenged
by Zabel
again Zabel, beaten.
And Mario Cipollini is back!

Stage 4, 1999

TWO SECONDS

These two riders have become the heroes of the day.
Everybody outside our commentary box is willing them on
but I think it cannot happen.
They are just behind them now
and I think they might even get picked up at the sign of
one kilometer to go.
There is always a psychological moment when sprinters
always look at one another and there's
a two-second hesitation.
And it's not going to happen.

Stage 4, 2003
On Stuart O'Grady and Robbie
McEwen breaking away then
getting caught before the
final sprint

BY A NOSE

Once he smells
the finish,
he will squeeze
that little bit more
out
of his body.

Stage time trial 19, 2002
On Lance Armstrong's
individual time trial

STANDING OVATION

He's going to give us
a very unusual
two-armed victory salute.
Don't fall off now,
that would be too embarrassing.

Stage 12, 2001
On Felix Cardenas standing,
no-handed, on his pedals as he
crosses the line

ONLY THE DAY

Cipollini is out of this
as Kirsipuu takes it on the line.
They said he wasn't the man for the big occasion
but he is now.
But he hasn't done enough to win the leader's jersey,
but he has done enough to win the stage.

> *Stage 1, 1999*
> *On Jaan Kirsipuu taking the*
> *stage win from Cippo*

BY THE HAIR

He's lost it on the line
only just

> *Stage 16, 1998*
> *As Jan Ullrich pushes just past*
> *Marco Pantani on the line after*
> *the two dueled up the Col de la*
> *Madeleine*

WIRE TO WIRE

This is the first-ever victory for Conti and it's going to be
one to savor
tremendous finish for him.
He's led all the way up Alpe d'Huez
from the minute of the breakaway,
he got on the bottom rung of the climb
and went clear
and now he's got the win.
And he can sit back and watch the rest
contest the Tour de France.

Stage 16, 1994
On Roberto Conti's stage win

ODE TO TRAFFIC

A bunch sprint!
This is how to do it
when you want to win.

Stage 5, 2000

ECK ACED I

No attacks of note all day
and now we're onto the Champs-Elysées and
the attacks have started.
Viatcheslav Ekimov, former world champion of the amateurs
       and now, of course, the defending world champion
       very shortly
          if he rides in the world championship of the pursuit
          over five thousand meters.
Let's just see how fast he is here.
This is a tremendous race for the line.
The field are boring down on him
he's got a real good chance though.
He winds it up.
       He won a stage like this last year
         when he went in the last couple of kilometers.
He keeps looking over his shoulder
that's an elementary mistake
       when you're out in front,
       you don't look where the rest are
       because there isn't much you can do about them.

You just go as fast as you can.

Across the Place de Concorde here, now, over the cobble-stones

he'll flick right very shortly then he'll see the finish here

and he looks good;

he looks really good

Ekimov could be picking off one of the most coveted stages

in any Tour de France

      to win on the Champs-Elysées.

> *Stage 21, 1992*
> *Ekimov will lose to teammate*
> *Olaf Ludwig*

ECK ACED II

Now, can he snatch any more

      at the finishing line

      as the riders break

      for the finish?

It looks

as though

a late sprint
by Viatcheslav Ekimov
will come to naught

Stage 2, 1996
As Ekimov is beat out of the
sprint by Mario Cipollini

ANONYMOUS

The sprinters are in a perfect place,
poised for the attack
as they start for the line
now.
And it looks as though Ludwig is going to come up on the
barriers.
Abdoujaparov can't get off his wheel
Olaf Ludwig gets the stage.
Nobody mentioned him.

Stage 13, 1993

LONGING

It's a long way
to the line.
You can't go
too soon.

Stage 21, 2000

DONNE & DONE

The bell
this time
and there's no tomorrow
in the Tour de France

Stage 20, 2001

FINIS

All that remains is
the traditional salute.

Stage 10, 1994

-V-

INDEX OF POEM TITLES

Doug Donaldson, a former maintenance, skills, and nutrition editor for *Bicycling* magazine, is also the author of *Bicycling Magazine's Guide to Bike Touring* and a freelance writer for publications including *Better Homes and Gardens* and *Men's Health*. Donaldson lives in eastern Pennsylvania and always hears Phil's voice on the longest, hardest climbs.